James Whitbourn

Son of God Mass

for mixed voices, organ
and soprano saxophone
(2001)

CHESTER MUSIC
*part of **WiseMusic**Group*

EXCLUSIVELY DISTRIBUTED BY
HAL•LEONARD®

The première of the *Son of God Mass* took place on 2nd June 2001 at St Mary's Church, Kippington, Sevenoaks, Kent. The Chantry Choir was conducted by James Whitbourn, with John Harle (saxophone) and David Goode (organ).

The main choral movements, which set the Ordinary of the Mass (Kyrie, Gloria in excelsis, Sanctus and Benedictus, Agnus Dei), can stand alone as a liturgical 'missa brevis', scored for choir and organ.

The other movements turn the work into a devotional concert piece and introduce the evocative sound of the soprano saxophone. In the concert version, the movements should flow in an unbroken sequence.

The whole work, including the meditative movements, has successfully been performed in the course of the liturgy. The additional movements can be used as follows:

Introit – Kyrie – Kyrie meditation – Gloria are used in sequence in the place of the *Kyrie* and *Gloria*. If an absolution is normally included between the *Kyrie* and the *Gloria*, this can be spoken by the priest at bar 32 of the Kyrie meditation over the quiet held chord but before the saxophone cadenza.

Lava me can be included as a meditation after the Creed, or, beginning at bar 9, during the distribution of the Sacrament. *Pax Domini* is heard while the Peace is exchanged. In this case, the Invitation to exchange the Peace may be made between bars 4 and 5, so that the fanfare introduces the Invitation.

The *Amen* may be used at the conclusion of the Mass.

Duration: circa 24 minutes

Son of God Mass is recorded by the Choir of Clare College Cambridge, directed by Timothy Brown, with John Harle (saxophone) on Etcetera KTC 1248 (*James Whitbourn: A Finer Truth*)

The saxophone solo part to the *Son of God Mass* is available on sale from the publisher, Order No. CH63272-01

Son of God Mass

JAMES WHITBOURN

Introit

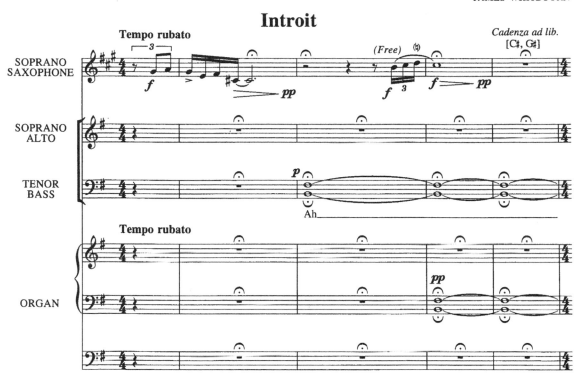

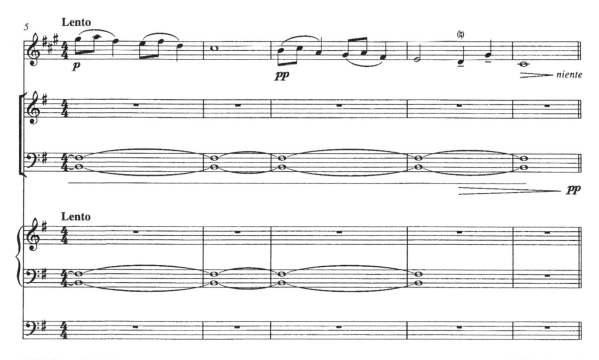

Kyrie

8

Ky - ri - e e - lei - son,

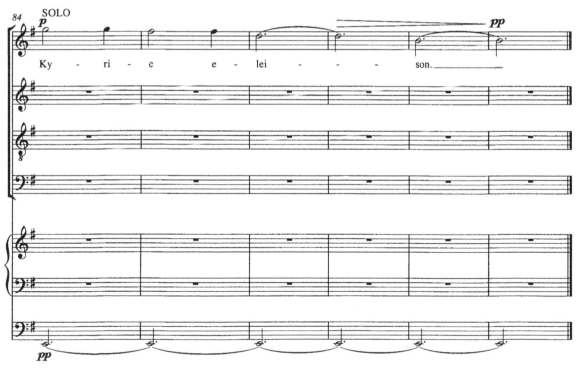

SOLO

Ky - ri - e e - lei - - son.

10

Kyrie meditation

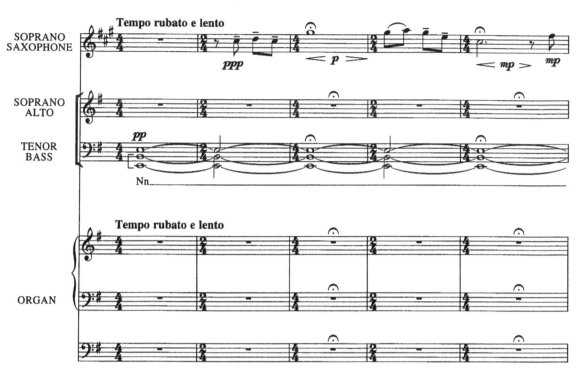

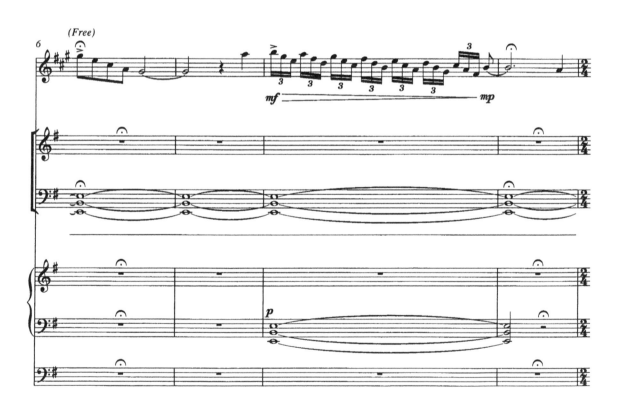

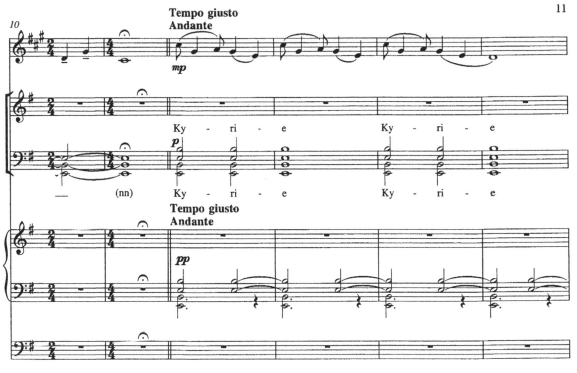

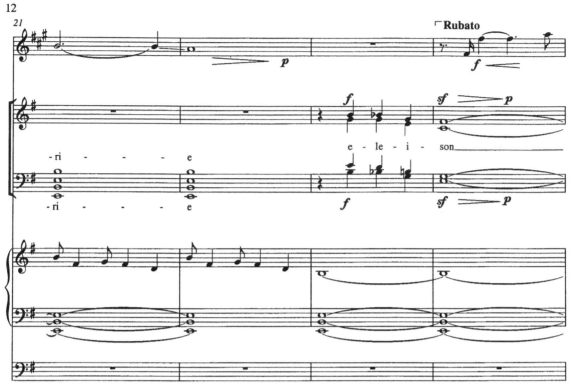

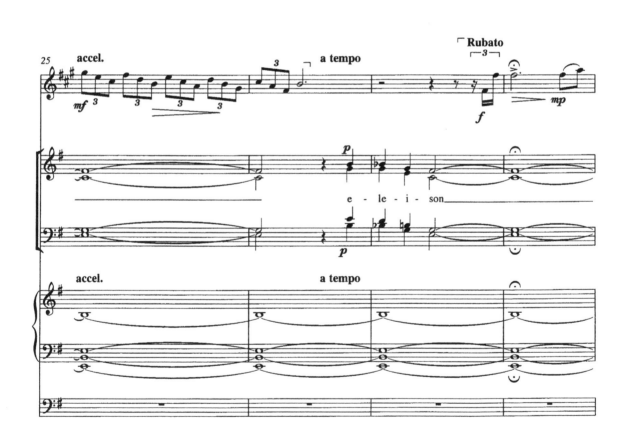

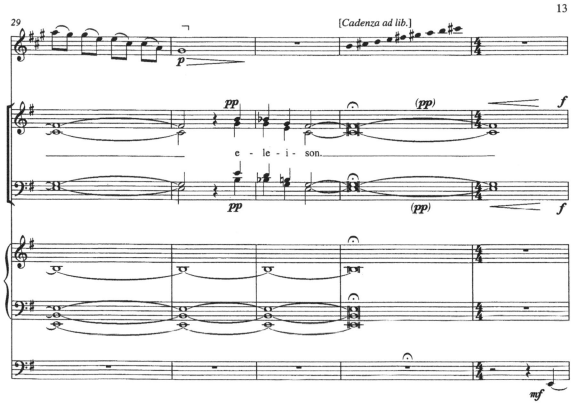

[Cadenza ad lib.]

e - le - i - son.

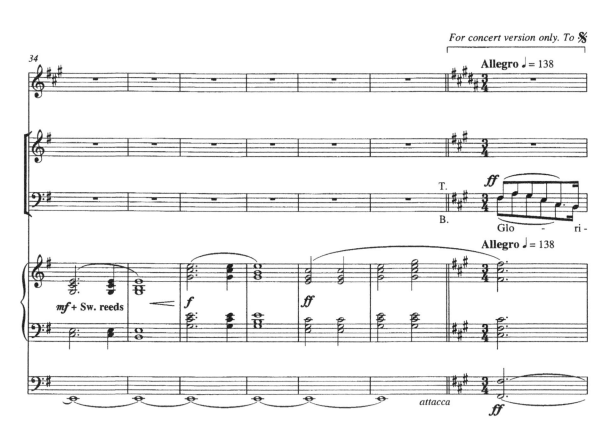

For concert version only. To 𝄋

Allegro ♩ = 138

T.

B. Glo - ri -

Allegro ♩ = 138

mf + Sw. reeds

attacca

Gloria

se - des ad dex - te - ram Pa - tris, mi - se - re - re no - bis.

se - des ad dex - te - ram Pa - tris, mi - se - re - re no - bis.

se - des ad dex - te - ram Pa - tris, mi - se - re - re

se - des ad dex - te - ram Pa - tris, mi - se - re - re

tu so - lus Do - mi - nus,

tu so - lus Do - mi - nus,

no - bis. Quo - ni - am tu so - lus San - ctus, tu

no - bis. Quo - ni - am tu so - lus San - ctus, tu

attacca
32' Reed

Lava Me

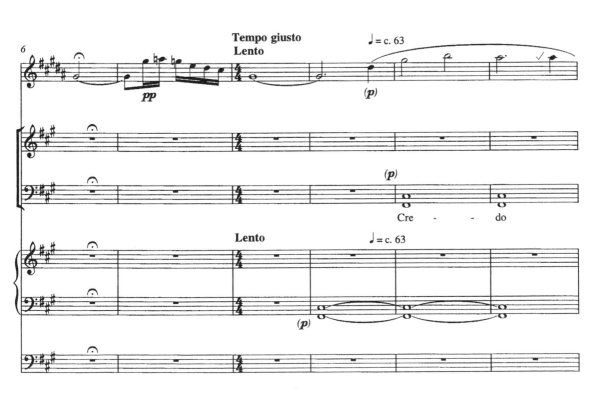

24

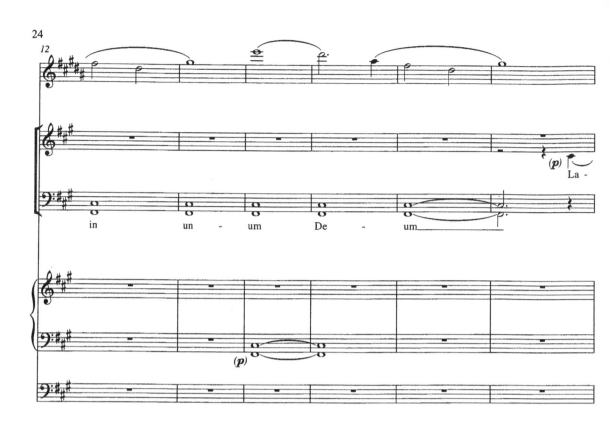

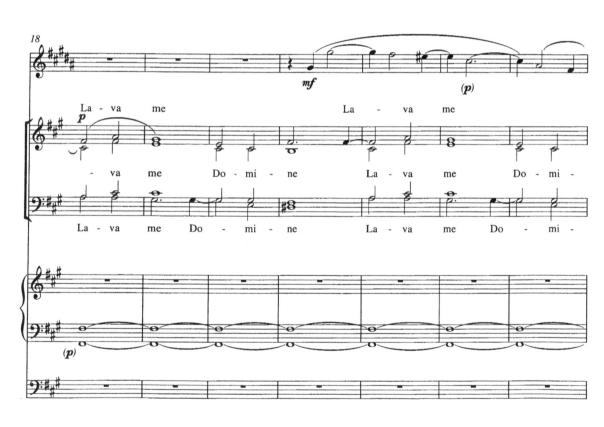

26

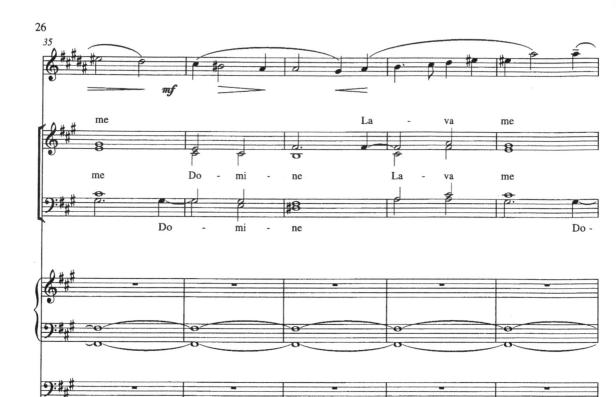

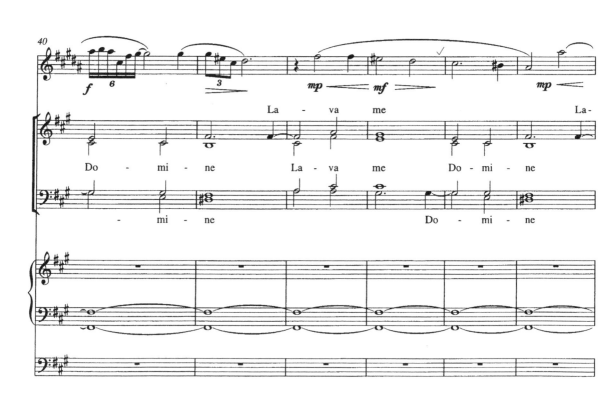

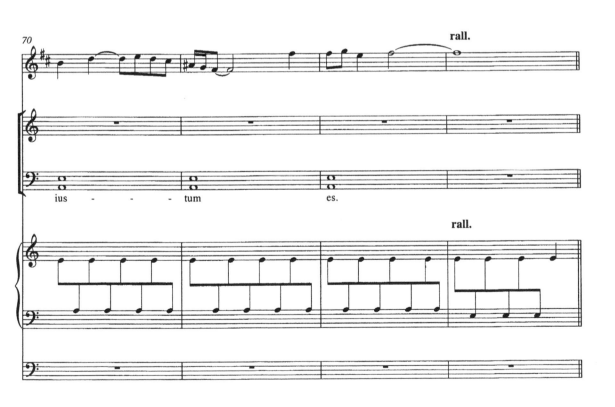

Sanctus and Benedictus

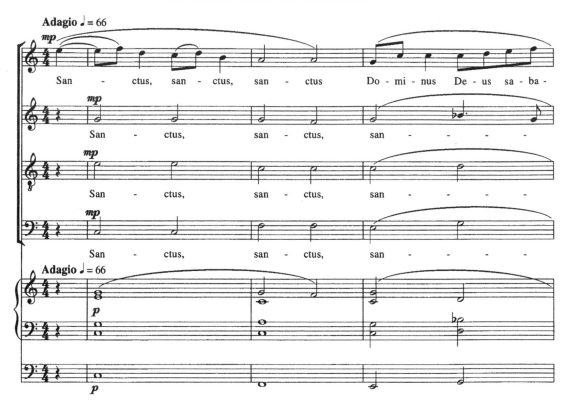

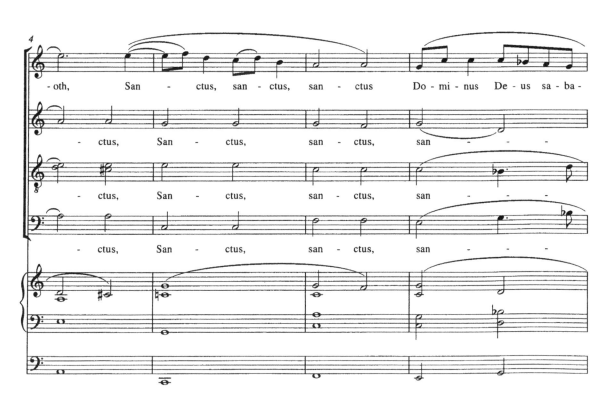

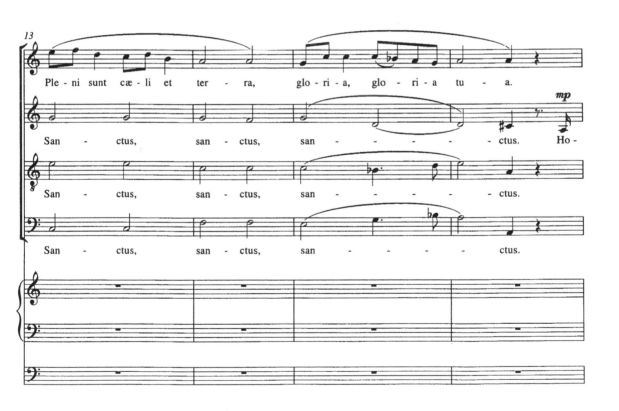

attacca

Pax Domini

38

Agnus Dei

tol - lis pec - ca - ta__ mun - di: Do - na no - bis pa - cem, do - na no - bis,__

a - - - gnus: Do - - na no - bis

a - - - gnus: Do - - na no - bis

a - - - gnus: Do - - na no - bis

do - na no - bis,__ do - na, do - na no - bis pa - - cem.

pa - cem, do - na no - bis pa - - cem.

pa - cem,__ do - na no - bis pa - - cem.

pa - cem, do - na no - bis pa - - cem.

Amen

* a few voices only

Easter 2001

1//07(60834)
Printed in England